D0266111

THE
SALESMAN'S
SHOES

THE SALESMAN'S SHOES

Tanka

James Roderick Burns

MODERN ENGLISH TANKA PRESS
Baltimore, Maryland.
2007

MODERN ENGLISH TANKA PRESS
Post Office Box 43717
Baltimore, Maryland 21236
www.modernenglishtankapress.com
publisher@modernenglishtankapress.com
www.thesalesmansshoes.com

The Salesman's Shoes

Copyright © 2007 by James Roderick Burns.

Some of the poems in this collection have appeared, or soon will, in the following publications: *Anon, Chanticleer Magazine, Haiku Scotland, Hummingbird, Lynx, Modern English Tanka, The North, Poetry Scotland, Ribbons, The Tanka Journal, The Poetic Image* (Birmingham Words Pamphlet No. 1) and *Tanka Splendor* 2006.

The front cover photograph by Walker Evans is from the Library of Congress, Prints & Photographs Division, FSA-OWI Collection, [reproduction number, LC-USF342-T01-008287-A DLC].

All rights reserved. No part of this book may be reproduced in any form or by any electronic or mechanical means including information storage and retrieval systems without permission in writing from the publisher, except by a reviewer who may quote brief passages, up to six tanka, in a review.

The Salesman's Shoes. Tanka by James Roderick Burns.

ISBN 978-0-6151-4396-5

for Caroline *and* Olive

In Memoriam
Jack Burns, 1917-2006.

Seeing traffic lights
sequencing through green, amber
red for nobody
the night watchman's heart blows out
like a torn bicycle tyre.

Along the roofline
between gaps in new shingles
down the builder's chute
and out into the chaos
of the rough yard—an orange.

The fall of the leaves
from their greeny-brown corners
as the tea bag's skin
grows ancient under my spoon—
dark, silent, inscrutable.

This end of the bridge
a fat worker rests his gut
against the railings—
driving past he is two men
tightening bolts, glancing up.

James Roderick Burns

From my landlocked desk
I stare through dirty windows
two office buildings
and a dark gash in the hull
at brine pumping like heart's blood.

New boots and a peach—
odd that the moment I feel
grit beneath my sole
is the moment I notice
my teeth strike against the stone.

In the corridor
the elderly salesman's shoes
wait despondently
like lizards on a creek bed
for some long-vanished polish.

Rush hour, the side streets
dark save for third-floor goldfish
behind bright windows
secure in the blue lagoon
of their seven second world.

The civil servant
breaking at nine twenty five
stirs discontentment
into papery coffee
like a dollop of fresh cream.

Eternal typist—
permanent secretary
stationed at dinner
behind a wretched nameplate
eyes up the blowfish sushi.

James Roderick Burns

At the white margin
of a rough map of the world
two gulls stand, hot feet
sinking through ice and blurring
the continent of Europe.

After your seizure
the sparkling city recedes—
I see a greyhound
ushered from a long black car,
don't know what to make of it.

Change of perspective—
scraped down a frozen windscreen
the goofy photo
on my security pass
acquires a wise beard of frost.

Throwing cheerios
into the teeth of a gale
while fat swans cackle
and my three year old turns blue
I give thanks this New Year's day.

James Roderick Burns

Nothing much changes—
mechanical fingers grope
at rows of bumpers
while saggy power cables
sit back, hum their approval.

Middle class at last—
after a blossom shower
fussing and tutting
over these sticky traces
matted into the footwell.

From the banking jet
horizon and summer moor
harden into glass,
steel milk tanker inching by
like mercury to the bulb.

Sweet watery yard,
silver cylinder idling
close enough to touch—
farm boy floats up the ladder
thinking of flying saucers.

Portobello storm—
in the bank forecourt wet palms
turned up to heaven,
balance slips limp as posters
after the revolution.

These diminishing
strings of e-mail messages
(will we or won't we)
build like squeezed concertinas
to a magnificent yes.

Legerdemain—seized
with the possibilities
I fold down my page
and walk through the library doors,
draw a rabbit from a hat.

Skidding to work, snow
between the cobbles—is this
light piercing darkness
or the passing of the soul ?
No, just snow between cobbles.

James Roderick Burns

Moods, fluctuations—
sometimes the stack of mailbags
by the post room door
seems like boiled sweets, other times
dogs in a Chinese market.

Through the harbour's eye
tanker and transatlantic
layer of cables
pass on silken waterways,
thread an ocean of static.

Remembrance of sins—
blind man at the T-junction
surveying nothing
as I breeze along in dreams
raises his cane forever.

On fresh-laid tarmac
by Welch's Quality Fish
the cottony hand
of an ear infection lifts
and I hear the bus singing.

James Roderick Burns

Ghost moon—all I want
from your cerulean world
is my wife and child
made comfortable, a swift end
to this bitter August heat.

I'm slipping this in,
love, between luminous skies
and ruminations
on the permanence of things
just to see if you notice.

Three nights in a row
with this sleepless child, my head
resonant and full
as a late pumpkin swelling
in radioactive ground.

The end of the world—
on top of smouldering shame
a damp warehouse wall,
deus ex machina crows
croaking somewhere out of sight.

How then to afford
another anthology?
Squeezing the lemon
from peel and pith and dry flesh
to (at last) the squeaking pips.

On the open deck
I swerve within airy feet
of a building site,
observe a beetle walking
along a second floor beam.

James Roderick Burns

Yielding to the will
of the barber, I incline
my head to the floor
where bears and snowy egrets
battle for supremacy.

Journey to nowhere—
frozen river buckles round
a couple of stones,
recalls in deadened silence
the time when we three were two.

Calculating odds
the actuary flicks on
his full-beam headlights,
longs to hold the missing child
in this empty brilliance.

Mid-January—
bald discarded Christmas trees
and stacks of cardboard,
black cat skittering across
a brand new ironing board.

Crazy moth barrels
round the paper shade, drops out
like a flake of soot—
I raise the window and smile
thinking of you dressed in white.

Through the thin cloth seat
of the auditorium
sudden vibrations
and snapping rivets, the mind
breaking free on bright steel wings.

Willowy gantry,
two workmen bending to drape
a *Swan Lake* banner—
filled with sunshine I reject
the obvious parallel.

In geography class
a bored skater cuts his eyes
to the curved gym wall,
toe-joints popping and longing
to carve the rim of the world.

James Roderick Burns

Multiplication—
hand on stomach, Miss Leckie
chalks up the numbers
as birds squabble and somewhere
two aircraft meet in a kiss.

Look across to Fife—
beyond the shit-studded wharf,
the filthy tugboat
working this stevedore's world
lies the faint glimmer of kings.

James Roderick Burns

Lighting up a fag
and idly scratching his arse
in the vast scrap yard's
wilderness of metal bones
stands unreconstructed man.

How wonderful—snow
bright and short-lived descending
with equal magic
on the couple from Iran
and our wide-eyed one year old.

James Roderick Burns

Caribbean drift—
the gold helium balloon
we nabbed from Pancho's
drops from the ceiling, taps past
like a pirate craving rum.

The ice cube explodes
in my glass of grain whisky
as ice sheets dissolve
under the polar bear's feet
and I sit twiddling thumbs.

James Roderick Burns

Eight o'clock eclipse—
as a lorry reverses
past the creamery
blades of shadow cut the curd
into moonlit rectangles.

Different Sundays—
out for nappies I notice
a gingerbread man
behind fuzzy cotton blinds
knocking back a few stiff ones.

James Roderick Burns

When after an hour
you appear in low-key style
between the butcher's
and the green neon bar sign
my heart empties like a vault.

Escaping at lunch
from the fairytale of work
I wolf my sandwich
turn the page and discover
three trapped crumbs, proud as tumours.

James Roderick Burns

On a scratched zinc shelf
in the theatre toilets
a red-eyed waiter
contemplates lines, finally
gets the manqué off his back.

Savour of hotdog
and overhanging bosom
and raw woody ink—
circles in the inferno
of this bookless passenger.

James Roderick Burns

Driving up country
in saturnine mood I pass
shallow-sloped fields, catch
a tractor carving the turf
into a wide cartoon smile.

Huge swan breaks away
from the isinglass river
and for a moment
we cease our disquisition
on this sharp world's splintered heart.

Outside the grocer's
shrink-wrapped phone directories
tower like icebergs
while lettuce and cucumbers
wilt in the unending sun.

Like a white tiger
or a stone fish on the reef
this dread siren song
from the staff restaurant walls—
ships, rippling seas, escape.

James Roderick Burns

Under his brittle
relentless anthracite gaze
the secretary
weighs up coffee on a spoon,
chemical compositions.

Ah, broken wiper
dragging smears across the glass
of the driver's side—
won't you now illuminate
the sound of one blade flapping?

James Roderick Burns

Summer infection—
queuing up for oranges
cracked ice in my bones
I wince then smile at the sound
of a shattering bottle.

Wading through papers
I cast the odd furtive glance
across the water
to the bosomy black lace
of crane-wiring against cloud.

James Roderick Burns

Four o'clock—I wake
from vertical dreams to sounds
of a creaking door,
find this slumbering gargoyle
between our two stone towers.

Driving to England—
morning gatherings of mist
along the valleys
knitting up, folding over
the pearl button of the sun.

James Roderick Burns

On my coffee cup
Warning—contents may be hot.
Beyond the terrace
a wren takes flight, instructions
stamped on the back of its wings.

Cathedral towers—
I borrow your camera
to snap the swallows,
lean back and press the shutter
as the last bird disappears.

What draws the fixed gaze
of this velvet assemblage
of luminaries
to the plinth-lined gallery?
Ah, ladies with their baps out.

The end of the day—
in an empty sky I see
slow roosting birds, dusk
like spilt molasses dripping
on the disappearing world.

Watching the spider's
meticulous clockwise turns
I shut down the plan
and wait for that first tremor
through my trembling keyboard.

Noon delivery—
seagulls rising and falling
on a bloody street
as trucks splash over cobbles,
passers-by cover their mouths.

James Roderick Burns

Scraping at windows
the newsagent's boy reveals
a faded Capstan
poster, my dead grandfather
lighting up behind the glass.

Though out on the street
a miniature digger
grabs at paving stones,
smashes its way to the mains
still water flows between us.

Seeing the oak tree
glowering and knotting up
its slow-motion fist
against a brick wall, I write
my resignation letter.

Hot stink of metal,
shrieks and the roundabout whoosh—
in this cubicle
how sorry I feel for you
my unfortunate daughter.

James Roderick Burns

Sharp speck of a crane
moves with unsteady purpose
through a dipping sun
like new life groping towards
the nourishment of the yolk.

In the urinal's
convex nozzle, a stomach
too huge to be mine—
somewhere a seven-foot man
runs through a hall of mirrors.

James Roderick Burns

Mourning characters
at the end of a novel
there is always this—
print ghosting on a blank page
and the smell of fresh coffee.

About the Poet

James Roderick Burns was born in the north of England in 1972 and grew up on the Yorkshire moors. He was educated at Balliol College, Oxford , and is the editor of a recent anthology, *Miracle & Clockwork* (Other Poetry Editions). He is currently enrolled in the Creative Writing programme at Oxford University and lives with his wife and daughter in Edinburgh, Scotland.

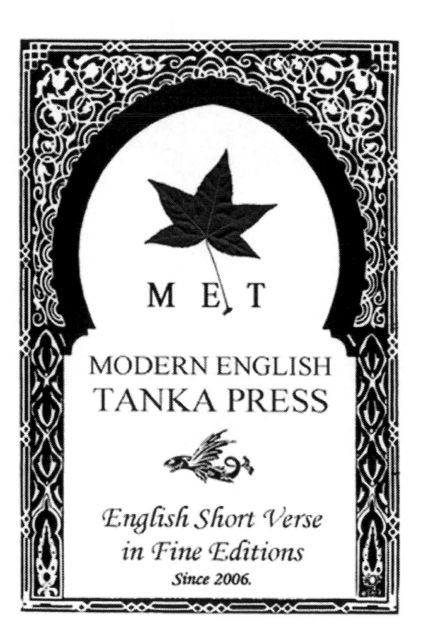

M E T

MODERN ENGLISH
TANKA PRESS

*English Short Verse
in Fine Editions*
Since 2006.

Modern English Tanka

Print Edition: ISSN 1932-9083   Digital Edition: ISSN 1930-8132

Modern English Tanka Press,
Baltimore, Maryland, USA,
publishes the quarterly journal of western tanka,
Modern English Tanka, both as a print journal
and in an online digital edition.
The best tanka poets in English
are to be found in the pages of *MET*.
Visit the *MET* website at www.modernenglishtanka.com.

Modern English Tanka Press maintains an online presence at
www.modernenglishtankapress.com.

TankaCentral.com

Sponsored & maintained by
Modern English Tanka Press

WWW.TANKACENTRAL.COM
is the internet megasite for tanka enthusiasts and students.

The mission of TankaCentral.com is to promote the tanka form of poetry, to educate newcomers to tanka about the form's history and future, techniques and uses, and to work for wider publication of tanka in both specialty and mainstream poetry venues. In order to accomplish this mission, it is our intent to build this into a megasite that will be the best place to study tanka on the internet, with its own onsite resources, with comprehensive links to other relevant sites, with connections to others who write, read, and publish tanka, and that can become the best source for finding places that publish tanka, calls for submissions, contests, etc.

SPECIAL FEATURES: Audio & Video of poets reading their tanka. Bibliographies. Links to organizations, communities, discussion lists, etc., for tanka poets. The Tanka Roundtable (a Google Group). The TankaCentral Blog. Submissions Calendar. Links to journals that publish tanka. And much more. If you love tanka, you owe it to yourself to visit TankaCentral.com.

Also from **MODERN ENGLISH TANKA PRESS**

The Five-Hole Flute

Denis M. Garrison & Michael McClintock, Editors
ISBN: 978-0-6151-3794-0.

THE FIVE-HOLE FLUTE affords the reader an impressively compact
and rich overview of modern tanka, cinquain, and haiku,
and of the changing shape and power of these forms
when arranged in sets and sequences.

The works in this exemplary collection offer a glimpse into the
extraordinary diversity and sometimes startling richness of the
modern short poem in English, and disclose a fascinating but hitherto
concealed dimension of literary creativity: the integration of
autonomous short poems into new, coherent, interactive patterns that
break free of the conventional stanzaic forms of longer narrative,
epic, and lyrical verse. Several techniques are illustrated—including
anaphora, thematic linking, antiphonal response, and more—
demonstrating the manifold possibilities for grouping tanka, cinquain,
and haiku in compositions that convey an expanded poetic experience,
a compound literature having broad scope and unlimited potential
for dealing with the many layers and complexities of
human experience, thought, and emotion.

Resonant with the breadth and vision of literary collage, mural, and
existential mandala, the short form poets of the twenty-first century
reveal cultural and artistic roots not only in the ancient Japanese
waka/tanka tradition, but equally in the subjective realism of the
Impressionist painters and the short works of such Imagist poets as
Adelaide Crapsey, the early Ezra Pound, T. E. Hulme, Amy Lowell,
H.D, and Wallace Stevens.

MODERN ENGLISH TANKA PRESS
is pleased to present readers with this compelling,
highly readable, unique anthology.

THE FIVE-HOLE FLUTE
Modern English Tanka in Sequences and Sets
Edited by Denis M. Garrison & Michael McClintock
Available from www.Lulu.com/modernenglishtanka or major booksellers.
Price: $13.95 USD. ISBN: 978-0-6151-3794-0. Trade paperback. 116 pages,
6.00" x 9.00", perfect binding, 60# cream interior paper, black and white
interior ink, 100# exterior paper, full-color exterior ink.

www.modernenglishtankapress.com
www.thefiveholeflute.com

Also from **MODERN ENGLISH TANKA PRESS**

Hidden River

Haiku by Denis M. Garrison
ISBN: 978-0-6151-3825-1.

"One wonders when they read the name of a man or even if they see his picture, what is he truly like? In my opinion, the best way to know a man is to study in depth what he puts down on paper. Denis Garrison would easily be recognized for the outdoorsman that he is by his haiku. Words and phrases such as: 'hidden river, plowed field, leafing orchards, hunger moon, old tin cup, rabbit spoor, river stones, bridle paths, spring-fed creek, woodpecker's vibrato, fragrant hay bales, sparrow tracks in fresh snow, field of ripe pumpkins, scorched dirt, cowpies, frog song and fireflies, woodcutter's cabin' and so forth, appear throughout his book. Denis skillfully gives readers a strong but pleasant taste of nature in this fine presentation via the many outstanding haiku found around every bend of his '*Hidden River.*' "

—— an'ya, Editor of *TSA Ribbons* and *moonset* journal.

"Denis Garrison is an excellent poet; a breath of fresh air. He understands haiku and, as an editor of literary journals and the owner of a small book publishing firm, he realizes that, like any art form, one must pay their dues; putting in time, study, practice, and hard work. . . . With a fresh voice, Garrison writes poetry that resonates, doesn't 'tell all,' and lingers in the mind after being read. . . . Garrison does not adhere to a strict 5/7/5 syllable formula. . . . Added to the haiku are good metre, more than one layer of meaning, and a unique way of viewing life. . . . This is the genius of haiku: using an economy of words to paint a multi-tiered painting without 'telling all.' Garrison does this well. His poetic canvasses only look simple. . . . however, level after level of meaning unfolds, calling to mind the way tones, tints, and simple brush strokes bring to life a sumi-e painting. Denis Garrison writes beautiful haiku. I recommend his new book, *Hidden River*, to all who appreciate the genre and to those who want a good model to emulate in their journey to becoming a better poet. His book will leave an indelible print in your mind."

—— Robert D. Wilson, Managing Editor of *Simply Haiku*.

HIDDEN RIVER
Haiku by Denis M. Garrison
Available from www.Lulu.com/modernenglishtanka or major booksellers.
Price: $15.95 USD. ISBN: 978-0-6151-3825-1. Trade paperback. 184 pages,
6.00" x 9.00", perfect binding, 60# cream interior paper, black and white
interior ink, 100# exterior paper, full-color exterior ink.

www.modernenglishtankapress.com
www.hiddenriverhaiku.com